Petals of Praise

by

Muriel Larson

MOODY PRESS
CHICAGO

ISBN: 0-8024-6474-2

1 2 3 4 5 6 Printing/LC/Year 95 94 93 92 91

Printed in the United States of America

Contents

1

Morning Glories

Bible reading: 1 Corinthians 1:26-31

But [he] that glorieth, let him glory in the Lord (2 Corinthians 10:31b).

Have you ever gone out to your backyard in the morning and noticed multicolored morning glories displaying their beauty? I have. And the lovely bell-shaped flowers have lifted my heart with joy and made me look up.

Whenever I see God's beauty in the glorious creations He has lavished upon us, I can't help but praise Him and rejoice in Him. And that is what "glory in the Lord" means.

7

In our Bible reading Paul shares tre-mendous spiritual reasons for Christians to glory in the Lord. He reminds them of how God redeemed them, though none was wor-thy. Then, like lovely many-colored morning glories, the things that Christ Jesus did for us who trust in Him as Savior are presented.

A *purple:* He revealed to us His divine plan of salvation that we might become chil-dren of the King. A *blue:* He clothes us with His righteousness, giving us right standing with God. A *white:* He made us pure and holy in His sight. A *scarlet:* He provided our ransom on the cross from the eternal penalty of sin and for present deliverance.

When we glory in the Lord about His beautiful creations and the wonderful things He has done for us, it fills us with love for Him. This love arouses in us a keen desire to please and serve Him, resulting in a life that glorifies the Lord. We then desire to win others to Christ, to help them become what He wants them to be and to enjoy the peace, joy, and abundant life He promised.

So each day in this devotional book we'll consider creations and blessings of God in which we can glory—and ways in which we can grow for His glory.

Lord, help me to reflect the glory of Your presence in my life.

2

Lilies: The Lily of the Valley

Bible Reading: Song of Solomon 2:1-7

I am . . . the lily of the valleys (Song of Solomon 2:1).

Most of us are familiar with at least several of the better known genera of the lily family. Daylilies in my front and back yards come up year after year to dress them with bright orange. Daylilies also come in yellow, pink, and red. Their tubers are said to make excellent eating, boiled and buttered. Their stalks, bloom buds, and flowers are edible also, prepared in various ways.

The fragrant white Easter lilies make their debuts around Easter. Plantain lilies are valued not only for their lavender, blue, or white clusters of flowers, but also for their rosettes of large, glossy leaves. Lilium produces the showiest blooms. All true members of the lily family are known for their trumpet forms. But many so-called lilies, such as the water lily and calla lily, don't belong to the lily family at all.

Lilies of the valley do though. After we moved into a house in Wyanet, Illinois, I noticed a large patch of lilies of the valley on one side of the house. One day I went out to check for flowers, and peeking through the leaves I saw stalks with tiny white bells.

Stooping, I plucked one and held it to my nose. Oh, such fragrance! As I marveled at the perfect little bells and their pleasant perfume, I gloried in the God who made them. Whenever I do this, I feel especially close to Him.

The Song of Solomon is considered a picture of Christ and His church—the Bridegroom and His bride—and their love for one another. The Bridegroom calls Himself "the lily of the valleys."

The flower referred to here may not have been the one we call that. It was probably some kind of lily that grew profusely in the valleys, however; and surely, since it is representative of Jesus Christ, it must have had the sweetest fragrance.

Jesus said that "Solomon in all his glory" was not arrayed like one lily of the field (Matthew 6:29). So there is no one more beautiful than Jesus in His love, compassion, and humility. Through His Spirit He clothes us with His beauty as we walk with Him day by day (Galatians 5:25). Do our lives exhibit the sweet fruit of the Spirit that can influence others for Christ? Can others see in us love, joy, peace, patience, kindness, goodness, faithfulness, humility, self-control? (See Galatians 5:22-23.)

Let us glory in our Beloved, our sweet and precious Lord Jesus—and seek to be like Him by yielding and allowing His Spirit to fill us and lead us!

Lord, let the beauty of Jesus be seen in me.

3

Crocus: First Volunteers

Bible Reading: Isaiah 6:1-8

If ye be willing and obedient, ye shall eat the good of the land (Isaiah 1:19).

Spring comes early in Greenville, South Carolina, where I live. Even so, I can hardly wait through the short winter for the first spring flowers to bloom. Although some forsythias and Japanese flowering quinces may bloom in January, the first individual flower up is the crocus. I've gone out some early February mornings to get the morning paper, and there, poking its head out from a light blanket of snow, will be a cheery, yellow crocus. How it thrills me.

13

Some Christians are "first volunteers" also. Without them many churches would fall apart. The church encounters financial problems: they are there with the money. The church needs various workers. "Here I am, pastor," they say. "How can I help?" Because of misunderstandings and disagreements, a cold blanket may fall upon the church fellowship. These Christians pray and work behind the scenes to draw their brothers and sisters back to each other and the Lord.

For many years now my main desire has been to glorify the Lord and serve Him. He has filled my heart with a great love for my fellow Christians. He laid it on my heart to be a "first volunteer." Each morning when I awake I report for duty: "Here I am, Lord. If there is anyone You want to reach or help, use me." So I am not surprised when someone calls me asking for prayer, seeking for counsel. Nor am I surprised when I am suddenly led to call someone, and that person exclaims, "Oh, I'm so glad you called! I needed someone to talk to."

This is the abundant life of joy and peace Jesus was talking about, and it is

something He wants every one of His followers to enjoy. It's really thrilling! Why not join
me as a "first volunteer"? It may cost you
something—but it will give you joy unspeak-
able.

*I am reporting for duty, Lord. Here I am
—use me!*

4

Yucca: The Spanish Bayonet

Bible Reading: Psalm 145:8-21

Thou openest thine hand, and satisfiest the desire of every living thing (Psalm 145:16).

Sometimes I get the impression that if I even get within five feet of one of my yucca plants, it reaches out one of its many sharp points and gets me. I don't dare bend over in their vicinity! I understand their name, "Spanish Bayonet!"

A semidesert plant, the yucca is the state flower of New Mexico. Its flowers are beautiful and fragrant, ranging in color from white to cream, yellow, or violet. They open at night.

16

That is no coincidence. For its propagation, the yucca depends on a tiny white moth that comes out only at night. In fact, this moth appears on the very night the yucca blooms. It carries pollen from one plant to another. Then the moth lays its eggs nearby. By the time they hatch, the yucca seeds have formed. Some serve as food for the moth larva. So plant and moth are interdependent. God, their Creator, made each for the other.

Could this arrangement have come about by accident or "evolution"? It couldn't have. From the very beginning of their existence these two creations had need of one another. They are just one more beautiful example of our Creator God's interest in every detail of His creation. God made these each for the other.

If God is concerned about every detail for those tiny moths and the yucca plants, think of how much more interest He takes in every detail of His children's lives. If He cares for little moths, how much more He cares for you!

Psalm 55:22 says, "Cast thy burden upon the Lord, and he shall sustain thee." As Christians, we can glory in our Father's concern and watch care over us. We can glory in the fact that He truly is our Father and has everything under His omnipotent control.

This is our Father's world. His eye is on the yucca moth; His eye is on the sparrow; and His loving, watchful eye is especially on you and all that concerns you. So fear not!

I praise You, Father, for your tender care concerning every detail!

5

Marigolds: Protectors

Bible Reading: Colossians 2:1-8

For I long to see you, that I may impart unto you some spiritual gift, to the end ye may be established (Romans 1:11).

The bright, cheerful looking marigolds have long been one of my favorite annuals. They bloom here in Greenville from May through October in just about any soil or situation. In the fall, when I clean up my vegetable garden, I scatter the marigold seeds around, and up they come in the spring.

Why do I grow them in my vegetable garden? Aside from the fact that they are decorative, they are protective. They rid the

19

soil of nematodes and Mexican bean beetles, and various harmful insects dislike them.

In addition, they are a natural remedy. Marigold tea made of solid yellow or orange petals settles nerves and helps a person to sleep if taken an hour before bedtime. Dry blooms may be dried further by laying them on thin white paper in a shallow box. Petals may be saved for tea or crushed and used as a herb in salads, omelettes, hamburger, and stuffing, and with roasts, beef, and chicken. Thus used in food, the petals are said to kill certain germs in the body. Mixed with vaseline or cold cream, they make a salve for wounds.

As I think of the protective qualities of this hardy plant, I'm reminded of the solicitude the apostle Paul had for his fellow Christians. He cared about their sorrows and burdens; he earnestly desired that they would be knit together in love and come to know and experience the riches of God.

How we Christians need to have that same solicitude today for our fellow Christians. In many churches less than 50 percent of those on the church roll attend. The others have fallen away for one reason or another. I am astonished, and saddened also, to hear how many marriages of Christians are falling apart. Our young people today are assaulted by temptations and devilish mind-defilers that many of us of the older generation never dreamed of, because in former times society as a whole upheld certain moral values.

Do we care what happens to our fellow Christians? I think that being a writer of personal experience stories has greatly burdened my heart for those who fall away. For I have heard tales of how badly lives, marriages, and children have been hurt in such cases. If we can just help one person keep from going astray, or help one to come back to the Lord, we might save a world of misery, or we might even save a life.

If you have not been a marigold type of Christian up to now—one who is protective of your brothers and sisters in Christ—why not ask the Lord to lay on your heart someone who may need your solicitude and help? We can help not only those who have fallen away but also those who need encouragement, comfort, and physical or spiritual aid. There are many of these in every church—

how we need more marigold Christians! Joy fills a marigold Christian's heart like a sunbeam.

Lord, help me to be a marigold Christian.

6

Roses, with Love

Bible Reading: Romans 5:1-11

We love him, because he first loved us (1 John 4:19).

When I was fourteen, a dark-haired, curly-headed boy sat behind me in my freshman homeroom at school. I think he liked my blond hair, green eyes, and rosy complexion. One spring day he brought in a beautiful, dark red tea rose and gave it to me. I smelled it, and its spicy fragrance entranced me. I think that's the day I fell in love with what is now the national flower of the United States—and also the state flower of New York, Georgia (Cherokee rose), North

Dakota (wild prairie rose), and Iowa (wild rose).

Traditionally roses have been associated with love and Valentine's Day. Many young men, and older too, have expressed their love for the lady of their choice by sending or bringing a dozen long-stemmed red roses.

God expressed His love for us by sending to earth the sweetest rose in all creation: His Son Jesus, the "rose of Sharon" (Song of Solomon 2:1). Matthew Henry says that probably the very best roses were found in Sharon, a fertile pastoral valley in Palestine. That Jesus here calls Himself the rose of Sharon, which grew so plentifully that it was considered common, indicates that the salvation He came to give us is a common salvation: it is open to all.

No Scripture expresses this truth so beautifully as the familiar John 3:16: "For God so loved the world, that He gave his only begotten Son, that whosoever believeth in him shall not perish, but have everlasting life."

When you think of or see or smell a particularly lovely rose, think of the rose of

Sharon, Jesus, and of His great love for you. He suffered and died on the cross for you and me that we might have our sins forgiven and live eternally in glory. Have you received Him yet as your own personal Savior?

Lord, forgive my sins. I receive you now as my Savior.

7

Orange Blossoms and Brides

Bible Reading: Song of Solomon 2:1-16

Behold, the bridegroom cometh (Matthew 25:6b).

Most of us tend to think of oranges in terms of a bright, round fruit. Since citrus fruits, and oranges in particular, are one of Florida's main crops and sources of income, Florida's citizens no doubt appreciated the fruit so much that they chose the blossom that precedes it as their state flower. But probably they chose it for its beauty, also, for orange blossoms have often been worn by brides.

Oranges are excellent sources of vitamin C, which is said to protect against all kinds of viruses, play an important role in all body functions, and contribute to good health and a feeling of well-being.

Since orange blossoms are connected with brides, let's think about that subject now. Most Bible scholars believe that the church, which is Christ's Body, is also His bride. I have never been drawn so close to my Lord as when I was reading Matthew Henry's inspiring exposition of Song of Solomon in his six-volume set. Try it—it's exciting!

Many Christians have probably wondered what this book is doing in the Bible. It takes on wonderful new meaning when we realize that the bridegroom is our Lord Jesus and we are the bride. Most of us have given lip service to this view when we've sung the chorus, reminiscent of the Song of Solomon (2:1; 5:20), "He's the Lily of the Valley, the Bright and Morning Star. He's the fairest of ten thousand to my soul."

In Matthew 25 Jesus tells of the bridegroom's return. Ten virgins awaited Him, but only five were prepared and had oil in their lamps. Only those with oil were allowed in for the marriage. Some believe this may be a picture of professing Christians: those who are saved and those who are not.

Unfortunately, many church members have never been born again—that is, they have never truly received Christ as their Savior; they have never been baptized by the Holy Spirit into the Body of Christ. It's so important that we make sure about this for ourselves. Have we ever really seen ourselves as lost sinners in God's sight and repented of our sins? Have we truly received the Lord Jesus as our personal Savior, and do we follow Him?

Jesus promised He would return to earth someday. Many believe that He may come any day now. For many this is a blessed hope. For me it has been a purifying hope. God promises a reward for all those who love His appearing. Why not read the Scripture again and see how sweet it will be? His banner over us is love.

Lord, may I be found ready when You return!

Lord, help me to be ready and waiting!

8

Poppies and Sin

Bible Reading: Ephesians 6:10-17

Submit yourselves therefore to God. Resist the devil, and he will flee from you (James 4:7).

I fell in love with the California golden poppy years ago when I lived in that state's Santa Clara valley. California's official flower grows wild by its highways, lifting hearts with its pleasant golden color. I'd never succeeded in growing this flower in another state until I sowed it here in South Carolina.

Poppies have an ominous side to them that is not betrayed by their varicolored showy flowers. Bruise them, and a disagreeable narcotic odor will assault your nose. Indeed, the white opium poppy is widely grown for the production of that painkilling and addictive drug.

During the nineteenth century many Chinese became slaves to opium, which British merchants brought from India. Opium produces agreeable dreams, profound sleep, and, in sufficiently large doses, death. In recent years many unfortunate young people in Western countries have been enslaved and killed by heroin, an opium derivative.

The poppy and sin are much alike: they present themselves as something pleasing to the eye, to the flesh. When Satan presented the first temptation to Eve, she found the forbidden fruit attractive to look upon and the ego-appealing promise of wisdom at its eating too tempting to resist. And usually when Satan tempts us, he does it step-by-step in ways that help us rationalize the way we're taking, because it gives us pleasure. Before we know it, we're losers.

Our Lord doesn't want that! In His Word He warns us against Satan's wiles. He also makes a way to escape. And He's always waiting for us with open arms to come to

Him, to repent and confess our sins, and to receive His forgiveness.

Lord, forgive my sins. Help me to follow You.

3/25/91

9

Forget-me-not: God Says

Bible Reading: Psalm 103

*The Lord is merciful and gracious,
slow to anger, and plenteous in mercy
(Psalm 103:8).*

Where did this romantic name for a
tiny, sky blue flower come from? Legend
says it is derived from the last words of a
German knight who drowned while trying to
retrieve this flower for his lady.

This delicate perennial is used widely
for ground covers in gardens, and it thrives
in temperate zones all over the world. Some
kinds are grown as annuals; others are noted
for their brilliant blue blossoms. The forget-
me-not is Alaska's state flower.

That German lady probably remembered her gallant knight for a long time because of his last poignant words. But there is someone else who is far, far more important to people all over the world than that nameless knight. And the marvelous things He has done for us cry for remembrance. Yet we forget our Lord and His benefits all too easily, don't we?

One reason God called David a "man after my own heart" was that David frequently reminded himself and others of God's benefits, and he regularly praised God for them. "Bless the Lord" means "Praise the Lord!"

How much closer would we be to our Lord if we started each day by praising Him for the tremendous things He has done for us. Look at some in that list in Psalm 103. The Lord forgives all our sins; He heals our diseases. He redeemed us from eternal damnation; He loved us even while we were yet rebellious sinners. He crowns us with love and compassion. When we delight ourselves in Him, He gives us the desires of our hearts. The Lord loves us with an everlasting love.

"My people have forgotten me," God says sadly of the Israelites in Jeremiah 2:32. And if truth be told, we for whom He died often forget Him and what He has done for us, don't we? We get so easily wrapped up even in such good things as going to church, fellowshipping on a human basis with Christian friends, working, tending to our families, and on and on. Our Lord gets lost in the shuffle.

So does our joy. Then one day, maybe, we wake up and ask ourselves, *What happened to that thrilling joy and spirit of praise I used to have?* Well, when something good isn't used, we don't benefit from it anymore. And if we have regularly put our Lord and praising Him on the back burner, no wonder we have lost our joy!

If that is where you are now, why now start glorying in the Lord and in all the wonderful things He has done for you? Get back your joy!

Lord, help me not to forget to praise You daily for Your benefits.

10

Mimosa: The Doer

Bible Reading: Proverbs 31:10-12, 20-31

Let her own works praise her in the gates (Proverbs 31:31b).

When I moved south, I fell in love with the mimosa tree, its graceful, tropical look, its glorious crown of pink, frothy blossoms. So I was delighted when one sprang up of its own accord in my flower garden.

I'll just let it get a good start, I decided. *Then I'll move it to a place in the front lawn.* And that's what I did. The tree grew fast —but another tree sprang up in my garden from the long taproot I hadn't been able to completely remove. After the first tree began blooming, I discovered the following

35

year that little mimosas were springing up all over the property.

Some of us Christians are like mimosas: we grow fast spiritually, we sink deep roots in our church, we scatter the seed of the gospel—and new Christians spring up. Like the foliage and flowers of the mimosa, the grace of the Lord and the fruit of the Spirit help us to show the world the beauty of Jesus.

Proverbs 31 indicates that a woman like this is well pleasing to the Lord.

I think the mimosa also provides a warning to us who are zealous for the Lord (and I am one of that number). The mimosa —with its seeds and diehard roots—has earned enemies because of its ability to take over a yard. I have had to learn to lay back in my witnessing and dealing with others. When I first came to the Lord, I'd jump right in strong on people. The Lord has taught me to wait for the leading of the Holy Spirit. I have found that that is the most thrilling and rewarding way to do things. I have learned, too, that I must be willing to allow the Lord to pull up my roots entirely and lead me where He wills.

We are not all the same in personality or ability. But each of us can, in our own way, serve the Lord and allow others to see Jesus in us.

Lord, may my life praise You wherever I am, in whatever I do.

3/29/91

11

Painted Cups: Survivors

Bible Reading: Colossians 1:9-14

*The Lord is the strength of my life;
of whom shall I be afraid? (Psalm
27:1b).*

I first saw the flamboyant painted cups
when we lived in the arid southwestern part
of Colorado. On our way through the mountains to Cortez, we stopped for a picnic
lunch. There blooming in a barren, isolated
spot were the gorgeous scarlet flowers I
came to know as Indian paintbrushes.

This flower, which is the Wyoming state
flower, lives in hard places; it fastens its roots
on other plants and draws its nourishment
from them.

Painted cups remind me of a dear friend who lived in a "hard place" for years. She first suffered crippling and much pain, then was confined to a wheelchair, and then to a bed because of her gradual debilitation by rheumatoid arthritis and the medicines she took for it.

Bea Fishter constantly looked to Jesus and drew her strength from Him. Thus, instead of complaining as others might in such a situation, she was a light to all with whom she came into contact. "My mother was a saint!" her daughter wrote to me after Bea's death.

What a blessing Bea was to me and to everybody because she refused to let the devil get her down with bitterness and resentment. Instead, she humbly submitted herself to the Lord. Because of that He used her greatly to His glory.

Some of us may get discouraged because the Lord doesn't chose to heal us or deliver us from a hard spot as He may others. Bea accepted the answer God gave Paul: "And he said unto me, My grace is sufficient for thee: for my strength is made perfect in weakness. Most gladly therefore will I rather glory in my infirmities, that the power of Christ may rest upon me" (2 Corinthians 12:9).

Lord, may I draw my strength from Thee; may Thy grace be upon me.

12

Magnolia: Evergreen

Bible Reading: 1 Timothy 6:6-12

For I have learned to be content in whatever circumstances I am (Philippians 4:11, NASB*).*

I first saw a green, leaf-covered magnolia tree after we moved one cold January from snowbound New Jersey to balmy Columbia, South Carolina. Then a few months later I noticed that its large, leathery, shiny textured leaves were dressed with gorgeous cuplike, waxy-white blossoms. I can understand why its scientific name is *Magnolia grandiosa.* This state flower of Mississippi and Louisiana has blossoms up to eight inches

New American Standard Bible.

across. Some magnolia trees grow eighty feet tall.

The flowers bloom in the spring, but usually by July new buds are forming and the tree stays green all year round. It's undisturbed by weather changes.

To me the color green stands for growing and life. Our Lord has given us as Christians the means for growing spiritually and enjoying the life of the Spirit. He imparts to us His grace and peace. By His power He has given to us all things that pertain to life and godliness through our knowledge of Him (see 2 Peter 1:3). Through these He has given us His precious promises, so that through them we may participate in the divine nature and escape the corruption in the world caused by evil desires. Thus we can keep growing no matter what happens.

Like the magnolia tree and the apostle Paul, we can remain undisturbed by changes in our environment if we stay contented with whatever our Lord provides. Contentment disappears when we crave things we can't have or when we covet what belongs to others. But with Jesus near we can be contented even in hard places!

Unpleasant circumstances reveal the stuff a Christian is really made of; the sweetness of Jesus can shine in dark places. The love, peace, and joy of the Spirit can make our faces shine like the green magnolia leaves do in January.

Lord, may I be content in You!

13

Goldenrods Go Everywhere

Bible Reading: Matthew 25:31-40

If any man thirst, let him come unto me, and drink (John 7:37b).

I grew up in Ocean Gate, New Jersey, a summer resort that had sandy soil, meadows, woods, and back roads. I loved the graceful goldenrods that grew wild everywhere during the summer, waving in the soft breeze from the ocean their cheerful, deep yellow flower heads. Apparently Alabamans, Kentuckians, and Nebraskans love them, too, because the goldenrod is their state flower.

These perennial flowers can grow in rather sterile soil. When I was younger, the colorful goldenrod got the blame that the less noticeable ragweed deserved for the hay fever many people suffered.

About a year ago an acquaintance of mine was suddenly struck by what Jesus said in Matthew 25:31-40. A Christian, she had always had somewhat of a tendency to look down on what she thought of as lower-class people: the poor, the dirty, the people of other races. Suddenly it occurred to her that Jesus had died for them too. It changed her whole attitude. Now she ministers as a part-time chaplain in an inner-city hospital.

I notice that most of us Christians tend to stay in our own little church clique, not particularly concerned about reaching out into our communities for Jesus. Well, Jesus reached out to the people thought untouchable by the religious leaders of His day. He was even given a bad name by them. But Jesus didn't care; He really loved those poor lost sinners. And many came to Him.

Let's ask ourselves the questions my friend asked herself: Are we visiting Jesus in prison, in the hospital, in rest homes? Are we feeding and clothing Him? Do we call Him on the phone when He is lonesome; do we visit Him when He is shut in? When we do these to His least follower, we do it for Jesus.

Isn't that a beautiful thought—that we can actually do such things *for Him?*

Put in my heart, Lord, a concern for others that will move me to action.

14

Sunflowers: All-around Workers

Bible Reading: 2 Corinthians 8:1-9

Therefore, my beloved brethren, be ye stedfast, unmoveable, always abounding in the work of the Lord, forasmuch as ye know that your labour is not in vain in the Lord (1 Corinthians 15:58).

The sunflowers, which are members of the daisy family, are absolutely amazing as far as their contributions to the welfare of man, bird, and beast are concerned. Kansas's state flower is a native of America. The Indians used the seed for food, ground it for meal, and extracted its oil for various uses.

Old World inhabitants, as well as New World dwellers, regard the roasted or baked sunflower seed as a delicacy, a great snack food. Health food enthusiasts love it, for it is extremely high in protein, calcium, phosphorus, thiamin, riboflavin, and niacin. Good cooks highly esteem its oil. Poultry growers use the seed extensively, because they have found that it results in healthier chickens. Wild birds also are partial to sunflower seeds.

One sunflower, the Jerusalem artichoke, provides tasty tubers, which are cooked and eaten as potatoes are. My neighbor made some delicious relish with hers and gave me a jar of it. I loved it!

Sunflowers grow tall and their golden-petaled blooms huge. As the heads grow heavy with seeds, the stalks sometimes need support. When sunflowers grow close together, they smother the weeds.

This long list of the all-around utility of the sunflower reminds me of some Christians I know. They are those who are known by all in the church for their usefulness in various areas of the Lord's work and for their dependability. Often if someone wants something done, he asks one of these persons. For if a sunflower Christian can possibly do it, he or she will!

I know why this is so, for it's something I've seen in my own life after I gave it all to Christ. It's the realization that if the Lord or one of His people ask me to do something, I should probably accept the privilege of doing it for the Lord. Now why do the doors seem to open for some people to do so many things? It's because they are willing.

Some years ago the Lord laid on my heart to go forth with my travel trailer and hold camper Bible clubs at state parks. I felt that would take more courage than I had. But because of my past experience with Him and His enabling power, I obeyed Him in it anyway. And oh, the blessings I have realized because I have obeyed! So many precious souls have come to know Jesus.

If a person will obey in respect to doing one thing, then the Lord will open the doors to other opportunities. But those who are fearful or don't want to put themselves out are among the majority of professing Christians who are missing the joys and blessings of walking with Jesus.

Some of us, however, may be doing God's will by supporting those who have many responsibilities in God's work. Some of God's most precious sunflowers are those who hold no office or title, but quietly and faithfully help in any way they can find. Among the greatest of these are the prayer warriors.

Thank you, Lord, for opportunities to serve You. Help me to be a sunflower Christian!

15

Black-eyed Susan: Sunshine Spreader

Bible Reading: 1 Corinthians 13:1-7

Owe no man anything, but to love one another (Romans 13:8a).

The black-eyed Susan is probably the best known yellow coneflower because of the prolific way in which it has spread from the prairies of the United States to its entire eastern seaboard. This cheerful-looking, golden, daisy-like flower dresses up the sides of numerous highways, the edges of lakes, and campgrounds by the seashore. A bienniel, it is the state flower of Maryland.

Farmers have found the black-eyed Susan difficult to get rid of once it is estab-

51

lished in pastures. But they have also discovered that since it will grow in barren places, it holds the soil in place until other plants can get a start.

We are blessed with a number of "black-eyed Susan" Christians in our church. Loving, smiling, and caring for others, these precious Christians spread cheer and encouragement among all with whom they come into contact. It's surprising and wonderful how catching this way of love is! Like the black-eyed Susan, it spreads among the folks at church and then reaches out to others in the community. Such love is missions minded. It impels us to pray, give, and go to the the lost in our area and around the world and share the gospel with them.

Our text says love is patient and kind, not proud or envious, seeks not its own, isn't easily provoked, and thinks no evil. It endures all things. (It's hardy, like the black-eyed Susan!)

Jesus has this kind of love and demonstrated it. The closer we draw to Jesus, the more we will be like Him—and the more real love we'll have for others. Do you know someone like this? Isn't it pleasant to be around such a person? Have you noticed how this person cheers and lifts others up and influences them for good? If you would like to be more like that, why not ask the Lord to fill you with His love and help you be a sunshine spreader, too!

Lord, fill me with Your love for others.

16

Columbine: Aquilecia

Bible Reading: Isaiah 40:25-31

I bare you on eagles' wings (Exodus 19:4b).

Columbines are among the most graceful and colorful of wildflowers. Their sophisticated and unique form, coupled with their five trailers, make them look to me like small, ready-made corsages with ribbons. The eastern species is a gorgeous combination of scarlet and yellow. They also come in yellow, red, white, and blue. The latter is Colorado's state flower.

When we lived in southwestern Colorado, we went for a picnic one day. Exploring on a barren, mesquite-covered plateau, we found a path leading down to a spring where there was greenery. And there in that lonesome place, growing among the rocks, were the beautiful columbines. What a treat!

Since the spurs of these flowers were thought to resemble the claws of the eagle, they were given the scientific name *Aquilegia canadensis*. The first designation is derived from the Latin word for eagle. So the columbine can remind us of the Lord, for in several places in His Word He is likened to an eagle who bares her young on her wings.

Several times in my life I have experienced the precious feeling of being borne by my Lord through a difficult time: when my father died and when my brother died. Also, I know He has borne me through many trials. Our text tells us to look up to our mighty Creator, to realize how great and powerful He is. It reminds us that He gives power to the faint and increases their strength.

When we wait upon the lord, He renews our strength. His Word promises that we shall mount up with wings as eagles, we shall run and not be weary, we shall walk and not faint. Though we live in rocky places, as columbines do, we can draw our strength from the living water Jesus has to give.

Lord, I will rest in You and Your strength and power.

17

Hawthorn and Trials

Bible Reading: 2 Corinthians 12:1-10

Christ also suffered for you, leaving you an example for you to follow in His steps (1 Peter 2:21, NASB).

Hawthorn trees come in anywhere from two hundred to nine hundred varieties; they're thorny, but beautiful. Related to the rose family, they are covered in the spring with showy white, pink, or red clusters of five-petaled blossoms. The hawthorn is Missouri's state flower.

After the flowers come shiny red fruits that resemble miniature apples. Most red haws are not particularly good to eat. However, they can be made into excellent jelly and marmalade. Mashing and brewing the fruit in hot water results in a tea that may possibly cure sore throats and correct diarrhea.

Because of their long, sharp thorns, impenetrable barriers can be made of small hawthorn trees. This makes me think of how the thorns of life may hedge us off sometimes from enjoying the blessings our Lord has for us. How may they do that? This is how: our thoughts may be so full of ourselves and our sufferings, as well as anger and questionings about why, that we may be robbing ourselves of the joy, peace, and abundant life Jesus promised His followers.

Perhaps you have wondered why God allowed something to happen to you or someone in your family, or why He hasn't answered prayer and removed a sore thorn in the flesh. Well, the apostle Paul prayed three times that God would remove his thorn in the flesh, but God didn't do it for this saint of God. He simply told Paul that His grace was sufficient for him, that His strength is made perfect in weakness. When Paul heard this, he began to glory in his infirmities.

Several years later Paul wrote his inspiring book to the Philippians, in which he told them again and again to rejoice in the Lord. Why did he do that? Because he had learned how wonderfully rejoicing in the Lord lifted him above his thorn.

Paul gloried in his infirmities so that the power of Christ might rest on him. Some of the greatest saints of God that I have ever known have been shining lights for their Lord especially because of their sufferings and the way they have accepted their limitations or pain. For in their sweet submission to Christ, the power of Christ is evident in their lives.

This life on earth is brief and so is the pain and suffering we endure. But the treasures we lay up in heaven will last forever.

Lord, help me to set my heart on heaven!

4/26/91

18

Violets: Root Strength

Bible Reading: Romans 6:1-14

Ye shall know the truth, and the truth shall make you free (John 8:32).

When I was nine, I found a big patch of purple violets in a park in West Orange, New Jersey. Gathering a big bouquet, I took it home to Mother. Ever since then, I have loved violets. My yard is full of them.

This pretty five-petaled blossom is the official state flower of New Jersey, Wisconsin, Illinois, and Rhode Island, and it comes in more than three hundred varicolored varieties. The pansy is one. The well-known naturalist Euell Gibbons wrote that violet flowers can be eaten raw and made into jelly. They contain more vitamin C than oranges. Cooked, their leaves taste like spinach; they're full of vitamins A and C. I use violet leaves in my sandwiches and salads, instead of lettuce. Though its flowers and leaves die each year, this perennial survives during the winter through its underground stem, which is full of stored food. In the spring it sends forth new foliage and flowers.

When we as Christians consider ourselves dead to sin, but alive to God in Christ Jesus, as our text advises, then our "old man" with all its dead works and fleshly control loses its power over us. Our "new man," drawing its strength from our root, our Lord Jesus Christ, will take control and spring up in newness of life and beauty.

Our Lord gives us certain principles for keeping this new man in control. He tells us not to allow sin to reign in our mortal bodies so that we obey its evil desires. Yes, we may still be tempted, but God's Word gives us the remedy: it says for us to offer ourselves and our bodies to God as instruments of righteousness. Romans 12:1-2 tells us further how to do this.

The violet's foliage follows cycles of living and dying; but if Christians obey Romans 6, the fruit produced by Christ's spirit will ever flourish.

Lord, I now reckon myself dead to sin and alive to You, and give You control of my life.

19

Mountain Laurel

Bible Reading: Matthew 7:21-27

The Lord is my rock, and my fortress, and my deliverer (Psalm 18:2a).

Mountain laurel lives on rocky slopes and sandy soils. I first discovered this fascinating bowl-shaped flower, with its distinctive circular design of ten stamens, when I explored in the woods surrounding Ocean Gate, New Jersey. The bushes grew wild in the sandy soil not far from the water. Connecticut and Pennsylvania claim the mountain laurel as their official flower.

This past summer I walked the shore of a lake in Georgia. The water was down, and

I could see the erosion water and weather had caused in the sandy banks. Then I came upon a great pine tree that had been under-mined and had fallen into the water. Along with other growth it had taken with it when it fell was a gorgeous flowering mountain laurel bush still sitting on its pad of earth. It was covered with pink-white blossoms. Its beauty made me sad, for I knew it would die.

The mountain laurel in its choice of sites reminds me of Jesus' story of two men, one who built on rock, and one who built on sand. When we trust in Jesus as our Savior, we begin to build the abode of our lives on the Rock. In Christ is security, strength, as-surance. Though the storms of life assail, we are anchored securely. We can trust in our Lord, no matter what.

If, however, we build our lives on the sand of this world, with little regard for our Lord's teachings and admonitions, we live in constant danger. Fortunately for us, how-ever, our Lord is always there with out-stretched arms, waiting for us to plant our lives firmly on Him, His Word, and His way.

Do you long for security? You'll find your greatest security in Jesus!

O Lord, my Rock, help me to build my life on You and Your teachings.

20

Clover: Trusting God

Bible Reading: Proverbs 3:1-10

Trust in the Lord with all thine heart; and lean not unto thine own understanding (Proverbs 3:5).

When I was a girl, I was superstitious about four-leaf clovers. I held the common belief that they were lucky. I would find and pick them and put them (of all things) in my Bible. When I came to the Lord and realized how pagan this practice was—and how utterly contrary to faith in God and prayer—I cleaned the clovers out of my Bible and threw them away.

But I still like clovers in general and let them grow all over my yard. They provide nitrogen for the garden, they make a good ground cover, and the red clovers especially are rather pretty. The red clover is Vermont's state flower.

Healing teas made with red and white clover flowers may be applied to external sores or taken internally as blood purifiers. Red clover tea is said to soothe the nerves, be good for bronchial ailments, and even perhaps heal cancer.

Our God has made many provisions for our well-being in this world. He has given us all kinds of good, nutritious food to eat—fruits, vegetables, dairy products, meat, and fish full of vitamins and minerals and other things our bodies may need. He has given us herbs for healing various ailments and emotional problems.

We can see these things, but unless we partake of them, their invisible benefits do us no good. Now some people eat nothing but junk food, and eventually they may pay for it physically. Others wisely try to eat well-balanced diets, avoiding things they believe might be bad for their bodies.

Both superstitious beliefs and trust in God require faith. But superstitious beliefs are like junk food: in a sense they fill a need, but they stand between us and genuine fulfillment. Complete trust in God meets our needs in every way. When we trust in our Father no matter what happens, without trying to understand in our own human way, then we have peace.

Often I have looked back at things that have happened—which at the time I could not understand—and I can see how wonderfully God worked them for good. Some things, however, I still don't understand, and I don't know if I ever will until I get to heaven. But one thing I know: I know Whom I have believed. And I know He knows so much better than I do what is best!

So trust in Him fully *right now*. Don't worry about understanding. Just pray and trust. He will take care of all the details!

Lord, I'm holding all my doubts and fears up to You, right now, and I'm letting You take them. I will trust You completely from now on!

21

Flowering Dogwood:
Christ's Sacrifice

Bible Reading: Isaiah 53

The blood of Jesus Christ his Son cleanseth us from all sin (1 John 1:7b).

My area in Greenville, South Carolina, could well be called Dogwood City, because in the spring the multitudes of dogwoods that line the streets bloom white and pink in all their glory. In the fall their leaves turn a gorgeous red. During the winter their red berries stand out brightly. I adore dogwoods; I have seven of them on my property. The flowering dogwood is the state flower of Virginia and North Carolina.

Perhaps you have read on an Easter card the legend of the dogwood tree. I think it goes like this: It is thought that the wood of the dogwood tree was used for Christ's cross—and that is why the dogwood never grows to be very big. In each flower's four petals (which are roughly in the shape of a cross) are what look like rusty dents, which remind us of the nail prints in Christ's hands. The dogwood's red berries are re-minders of the blood Jesus Christ shed for our sins. To me the white flowers stand for the way Christ's blood cleanses us of sin and makes us white as snow in God's sight. It's also interesting that this tree blooms in the spring, when our Lord was crucified.

I believe it is good for us to meditate from time to time on the tremendous sacri-fice our Lord made for us. It reminds us of His love and convicts us of carelessness and slothfulness in our Christian lives.

Consider these things. When Peter tried to protect Jesus from being arrested, Jesus told him that if He wished He could call ten thousand angels to His rescue. Jesus went through all that torture and suffering because of His love for us. He knew it was the only way we could be forgiven and saved.

Most of us think of the horrible physical suffering Jesus went through: the crown of thorns, the vicious lashings, the incredible pain of crucifixion. We also may realize the awful psychological torture He endured: the trumped-up trial that He was dragged to early in the morning; the lying testimonies; the mocking; the rejection by His people; the betrayal, desertion, and denial by those closest to Him; the shame of death by crucifixion.

Let me share with you what I think must have been the worst suffering He willingly underwent for you and for me. When our sins fell upon His shoulders there on the cross, our Lord Jesus cried out, "My God, my God, why hast thou forsaken me?" (Mark 15:34*b*). For the first and only time in all eternity, God the Father and God the Son were separated—because of our sins. Oh, to me that is love beyond understanding!

Now if God the Father and God the Son love us *that* much, how in the world can we help but truly love Them with all our hearts, souls, and minds? How can this great truth not affect every part of our lives and thinking?

Would it not help us to stay close to our Lord Jesus if we thought of the dogwood, and then reminded ourselves of Christ's love and sacrifice? That reminder will also help us to have faith that our loving Lord is with us through every trial of life. Jesus cares, He really cares.

Lord, help me to remember how much You love me!

22

Lilacs and Anointing

Bible Reading: 1 John 2:18-29

Now He who establishes us with you in Christ and anointed us is God (2 Corinthians 1:21, NASB).

The group of shrubs and small trees that bear the beautiful and fragrant flowers we call lilacs belong to the olive family. They thrive in full sun and slightly acid soil that is well fertilized and mulched, but they don't like wet feet. Lilacs bloom on last year's wood. The lilac is New Hampshire's state flower.

A related member of the same family is well known by its basic name: olive. It is, of course, the edible branch of the family, and its oil has many uses. According to the Bible, the oil was used in baking wafers used in sacrifice to God, as a healing lotion, as a cosmetic, to provide light, and for the anointing of priests and kings.

Now the apostle Peter told Christians that they were a "royal priesthood" (1 Peter 2:9). According to the apostle John, we who have received Christ as our Savior have received a special anointing of the Holy One that opens our eyes to the truths of God. John also reported that Jesus said, "But the Helper, the Holy Spirit, whom the father will send in My name, He will teach you all things" (John 14:26, NASB).

I have found a wonderful thing: almost invariably most of my true brothers and sisters in Christ, regardless of denomination, believe the same as I do concerning the major doctrines and teachings of God's Word. We may differ on some points, however. I think that may be because of a tendency of some to cling to old conceptions, as well as the willingness of others to be open to the teaching of the Holy Spirit.

How God has blessed us, to send the Spirit to dwell in us (and through Him the

Father and Son do, too)! Those Christians who aren't aware of God's living in them miss so much. When we are aware, then we are sensitive to His leading. If we are about to be led astray by false doctrine, the Holy Spirit will nudge us and lead us to Scripture. If someone needs our help, the Holy Spirit will lay on our hearts to call or write that person.

This beautiful truth is so real to me that I try to keep alert each day for His leading. He and I have had so many beautiful adventures together; and every time we have another experience of working together to help or reach people, I am altogether thrilled.

After all, a priest is someone who acts as a mediator between God and man. Since every one of us Christians is an anointed priest, according to Peter, every one of us has that amazing assignment. Every Christian is a special person, important in God's sight. Regardless of what anyone else thinks, that truth should lift our hearts.

Lord, help me to be aware of the teaching and leading of Your Spirit.

5/20/91

23

Anemone: Paschal Flower

Bible Reading: Matthew 28:1-20

*Christ died for our sins . . . and . . .
rose again the third day (1 Corinthians 15:3-4b).*

Anemones, also known as windflowers,
are hardy perennials that make attractive border plants in gardens. Their eighty-five species come in red, white, blue, and purple
shades. The anemone called the American
pasqueflower produces a showy, cup-shaped
blossom that consists of purple, violet, or
white sepals surrounding golden centers. It
is South Dakota's state flower.

This particular flower is also known as
"paschal flower," because it blooms around
Easter. The word *paschal* comes from the

Hebrew word for the Passover and was adopted by Christians to refer to Easter. The Hebrews' paschal lamb was that which was slain and eaten at the Passover; hence our Lord Jesus Christ is called the paschal lamb, since He was slain for our sins and we partake of Him when we receive Him as Savior.

Christ's death for our sins and resurrection for our justification are the two basic facts of the gospel (1 Corinthians 15:3-4). According to Romans 10:9, believing in our hearts that Christ was raised from the dead is necessary for our salvation, for His resurrection from the dead signaled God's acceptance of His sacrifice for our sins.

Our Lord Jesus Christ is no longer on the cross. He is no longer in the grave. We serve a risen Savior, one who returned to heaven in His glorified body to intercede for us and prepare a place for us who follow Him. Through the Spirit, Jesus also indwells and is always with His followers.

These are precious truths in which we can rejoice. Believing them, our hearts may be filled with faith, peace, and joy.

I praise Thee, O Lord, that You are my living, loving Savior!

24

Carnations: God's Bouquet

Bible Reading: 1 Peter 3:1-13

*By this shall all men know that ye
are my disciples, if ye have love one
to another (John 13:35).*

Because of its sweet perfume and ruffled beauty, the carnation is often used in
floral bouquets. I chose white carnations for
my bridal bouquet, and we often see them in
bouquets at church or send them to loved
ones. Another reason these gorgeous flowers
are used in bouquets is that they last longer
after they are cut. Ohio chose the scarlet carnation as its state flower.

Just as carnations make fragrant and
beautiful bouquets for homes and churches,

so can God's family. If Christ is the head of a house, that family can bloom sweetly before others. A young woman told me of the influence such a family had on her. She came to know the Lord through this family that was so different from her own. Then she longed and prayed that her family would come to Him, so that they would be like that other family. As she witnessed, her brother, sisters, and finally her parents came to Christ. Dad stopped drinking, and Mom's bad language disappeared. Now her family blooms sweetly for Christ.

The same can be true of a church family. As visitors and outsiders see the love and caring we have for one another, they will desire what we have. This love will also make them feel at home when they visit our church or some meeting at it, for hospitality is part of a genuinely Christian family.

When we moved into a new neighborhood in Dallas, a woman member of a local fellowship brought us a fresh-baked lemon-meringue pie; and when I had my baby a month later, she brought us more goodies. I was very impressed by this Christian woman and thought her church family must be very special.

Lord, help my family, church, and me to bloom sweetly for You. I rejoice in the privilege we have of doing so.

25

Mistletoe and the Tongue

Bible Reading: James 3:1-13

Let the words of my mouth, and the meditation of my heart, be acceptable in thy sight, O Lord, my strength and my redeemer (Psalm 19:14).

The mistletoe, Oklahoma's state flower, has yellow flowers followed by white berries. It's perhaps best known for its Christmas connection with kissing. The American kind may cause the blood pressure to rise. One elderly lady said she knew this was true, because when she was a girl she had often experienced a rise in blood pressure by standing under it!

Mistletoe is like the little girl with the curl on her forehead: when it is good, it is very good; when it is bad, it is horrid. Mistletoe is a parasite, drawing its nourishment from the trees on which it grows. The western dwarf mistletoes are called "slow killers." Their roots invade their host trees, stealing nutrients and water and eventually killing them. This plant shoots out its seeds as far as sixty feet. Wherever they land, up springs another plant. The common mistletoe is not so bad, unless it takes over a tree.

Now for the good side: According to some pharmacologists, American mistletoe produces a rise in blood pressure and can be used as a circulatory and uterine stimulant. European mistletoe is said to reduce blood pressure. Mistletoe is an excellent remedy for cholera or St. Vitus's dance and serves as a good nerve tonic. The plant may be brewed in hot water to make a tea.

Like the mistletoe, there is a good side and bad side to our tongues. The tongue can be used to spread rumors, to cause dissension and church splits, to wound, to curse, and to ruin relationships. Or it can be used to God's glory: to praise Him in prayer and to others, to encourage and lift up, to bless and help, to spread the gospel, and to heal relationships.

All of us know how easily our tongues can get out of hand. Before we know it we may slip and share a choice piece of gossip or say a cutting word. How can we control these rascally members? Well, I feel so keenly about using my tongue properly as a Christian that each morning when I awake I say the Scripture verse listed for this devotional.

The meditations of our hearts have a lot to do with what comes out of our mouths. If we think bitter, resentful, angry thoughts, they'll come out in words sooner or later. If we think about our Lord and our fellow Christians, and how much we love and care for them, that will come out in beautiful words.

If things you have said in the past have troubled you, perhaps you would like to have more control in the future and be a blessing to others. If so, why not start your day as I do? It helps a lot.

Lord, help me to guard my thoughts and words.

5/31/91

26

Yellow Jessamine

Bible Reading: John 15:1-8

God is no respecter of persons (Acts 10:34b).

The yellow jessamine (also called yellow jasmine) is a beautiful wild vine that thrives in the southern states of America. It climbs up tree trunks, creeps over the ground, and trails over bushes. Its large attractive flowers, which bloom in March and April, are of tubular-funnel form and anywhere from one to two inches in length. The yellow jessamine is South Carolina's state flower.

The way the yellow vine travels up and down and everywhere makes me think about our Lord Jesus, who called Himself the true vine, ministered to all kinds of people. He laid His hand on the feared lepers and healed them. He visited and ate and drank with the despised publicans and tax collectors. Among those whose lives He touched and changed were the former demon-possessed harlot Mary Magdalene, Nicodemus the religious leader; the rich man Joseph of Arimathea; and a bunch of rough fishermen whom others considered unlearned and ignorant. Certainly our Lord was no respecter of persons.

The Holy Spirit later led the learned apostle Paul to write, "Whosoever shall call upon the name of the Lord shall be saved" (Romans 10:13). So Jesus Christ and His way of salvation is open to all.

The Lord Jesus honors those of us who follow Him by calling us branches in Him. He desires for us to abide in Him and thus bear fruit. I believe He would have us to reach out even as He did to all kinds of people, bringing the way of salvation, leading them to Christ, helping them.

Let us not be surprised if, when we do bear fruit, we also experience trials. Those are the pruning shears that cut off the suckers of self on us, thus enabling the power of Christ to surge through our lives and produce more fruit. Looking back over my life, I find that I am grateful for those pruning times. I can clearly see how they drew me closer to my Lord and prepared me to be of greater service to Him. At the time I was going through them, it was rough and perhaps painful (a cut always hurts). But now I praise Him for His perfect pruning. The omnipotent husbandman knew just what I needed.

Look back on your own life. Can you see how pruning times brought you closer to the Lord and taught you many important lessons?

Lord, I praise You for all You have done or allowed in my life. When You are working on me, help me to trust You and keep on rejoicing in You, even as the apostle Paul did!

27

Oregon Grape and Good Addition

Bible Reading: 2 Peter 1:2-11

But grow in grace, and in the knowl-edge of our Lord and Saviour Jesus Christ (2 Peter 3:18a).

The Oregon grape, of the *Mahonia* ge-nus, is a spring-blooming shrub that pro-duces sweet-smelling yellow blooms in pretty racemes. This plant may grow to eight feet or more, and its blossoms are followed with small blue edible berries that resemble little grapes. It is Oregon's state flower.

What is a raceme? I asked myself. *If I don't know, perhaps others will wonder.* So I looked it up. A raceme is the type of flower-ing where blossoms on the same slender stalk bloom in succession toward the top. Immediately Peter's advice for spiritual growth came to my mind: how we should diligently add to our faith, virtue; to virtue, knowledge; to knowledge, self-control; to self-control, perseverance; to perseverance, godliness; to godliness, brotherly kindness; and to brotherly kindness, love (see 2 Peter 1:5-7).

Just as the blossoms open up along the stalks of the Oregon grape, blessing the eye with more and more beauty, so as Christians add the above qualities to their character, do they become more and more beautiful in God's sight and man's. That may be why some older saints we know may appear to be particularly beautiful. Godly character shows in a person's countenance, words, and actions.

Just for a minute or two meditate on Peter's list. If you haven't all the listed blossoms in your life, why not start making a diligent effort to add them one by one with the Lord's help? (We can't do anything without His help.)

Lord, help me to be virtuous. Help me to understand Your Word and hide its wisdom in my heart. Help me to exercise self-

control. Help me to develop patient endur-ance and godliness. May I exercise brotherly affection and Christian love. I rejoice in how You will help me grow more like Jesus.

6/8/91

28

Pinecone and Tassel

Bible Reading: Genesis 2:18-25

*So God created man in his own im-
age, in the image of God created he
him; male and female created he
them (Genesis 1:27).*

When I saw what Maine's state flower
was, I thought, *Well, that is one state "flower" I will have to omit. Whoever heard of a
pinecone being a flower?*

I thought I knew everything there was
to know about pine trees and cones. After
all, didn't I grow up in New Jersey's pine
country? Wasn't my hometown surrounded
by a pine forest? In all my walks through
those woods I had never seen a pinecone

flower—only cones that had fallen from the lofty trees.

I decided to give this one the benefit of the doubt and look it up in one of my encyclopedias. After all, Maine residents might not like it if I left their flower out. And I hereby apologize, Maine folks. To my surprise, I found you did choose a flower, and a unique double one at that. Maine's white pinecone and tassel consists of pollen-filled male blossoms that cluster around new growth on lower branches—and small, pink female ones higher up on the tree.

These flowers uniquely reflect God's arrangement for man and his propagation and companionship. He didn't make Adam and Ethan; He didn't make Alice and Eve; He made a man and a woman who complemented one another.

God made men and women different. Our mixed-up society today, however, tries to jam them into a unisex mold, planting this seed even in grammar schools. Some women have become militant; some men have become resentful of women.

As Christians, however, we can rejoice in God's two-sex plan and recognize that He has blessed both men and women with intelligence and many abilities. Both are important to each other and the children they produce. Whatever God has made us, let's be content to be that. And let us glory in the fact that if we are children of the King, we are princes and princesses in His sight!

Lord, help me to appreciate what I am, especially the privilege of being a member of Your royal family.

29

Sagebrush: Wilderness and Rest

Bible Reading: Numbers 13:16-33

For we which have believed do enter into rest (Hebrews 4:3a).

Nevada's state flower, sagebrush, is another state flower I puzzled over. But having traveled through the wilderness of Nevada several times, I can understand why they chose the sagebrush. This hardy shrub grows abundantly in Nevada, covering thousands of square miles there and in the arid lands to its north, east, and south. I can understand how seeing the dusky green sagebrushes covered with their fragrant yellow flowers in the fall would thrill many a desert traveler! The sagebrushes' leaves provide food for many small mammals and birds that live in its arid homelands.

After God delivered the Israelites from slavery in Egypt, He led them through the wilderness of the Sinai peninsula. He protected them and brought them safely to the border of the Promised Land, the land flowing with milk and honey that He had promised them—the land of rest.

The Israelites sent men forth to spy out the land. The men brought back luscious fruit, along with the report that the land indeed was what God said it was. But ten of the twelve spies also fearfully said there were giants in the land, and with their evil report they planted fear in the hearts of the people. When Joshua and Caleb tried to urge the people to trust and obey the Lord, the people threw rocks at them.

So in unbelief the children of Israel turned their backs on the land of rest God wanted to give them—and ended up spending the rest of their lives wandering around in the wilderness. Only Joshua and Caleb and the generation that grew up in the desert lived to dwell in the promised land of milk and honey and rest.

The writer of the book of Hebrews gave this as an example to the Jewish Christians that he wrote to, because a number of them continued to be zealously attached to Jewish Temple rites and animal sacrifices. Now that Christ had come and provided the perfect sacrifice for sin, those things were no longer necessary. Christians are to live by faith. When they do so, they no longer trust in their own works, but in Christ's finished work for them and in them. Thus they enter Christ's rest.

I suspect that sometimes we get so caught up in establishing our own righteousness that we forget that it is God working in us who makes us holy. Becoming a righteous person is not a matter of straining or legalism; it is a matter of resting and obeying the Spirit. Then it is a joyful experience.

When we walk with the Lord and obey His leading and Word, then our lives become what they should be in His sight, and we'll be happy Christians at rest.

Lord, help me to rest and trust completely in You.

30

Bitterroot and Backsliding

Bible Reading: Hebrews 12:5-15

Let us lay aside every weight, and the sin which doth so easily beset us (Hebrews 12:1b).

Bitterroot, also known as *Lewisia rediviva*, grows in the Rocky Mountains, and appropriately enough, it is Montana's state flower. A member of the purslane family, it has handsome pink flowers and does best growing in crevices in lime free soil. Its foliage dies down after it flowers.

The Bible speaks of a bitter root. Hebrew Christians were urged to look after one another, so that no one would fail to secure God's grace. This advice was coupled with the warning to watch out lest a root of bitterness spring up and hurt many spiritually.

I have seen that happen and have sadly observed how it operates in churches. One or more Christians may feel offended or hurt in some way. They will brood over the matter and become bitter. Invariably this results in "sour grapes" remarks to others, which may affect them, too. Before long, half the people in the church are infected by the bitter root. I've seen churches torn asunder by it, and many Christians fall by the wayside.

What can we do about a bitter root? Every one of us at one time or another finds himself belittled or overlooked. As a church musician and Bible teacher, I've had to deal with this myself. But I have learned to take everything to the Lord, knowing full well how bitterness can rob a person of peace and joy. In most cases, our pride is involved. Well, the Lord has shown me I am to forget myself and my pride; forgive, love, and pray for the person who has hurt me; and leave everything to my Lord.

On a recent occasion when I did this, I was thrilled by the peace my Lord gave me in the particular situation, and I've been able to live with and in it and actually keep rejoicing in Him. Through rejecting the root of bitterness this time, I believe I have learned a new facet and blessing of humility.

Our Scripture encourages us to look after our fellow Christians also in respect to roots of bitterness. When a fellow Christian begins speaking bitterly about some other Christian or situation that makes him angry, we may be able to help that brother or sister in a gentle way as the Spirit leads.

Such matters need to be handled delicately, but I've found that often the best way is to appeal to the person's own best interests, by pointing out how much holding such thoughts will hurt him or her. In one case, where I found a sister offended by another sister, I encouraged her to call that sister up and talk it out. The breach was healed, and they became the best of friends after that.

Roots of bitterness defile us with anger, hostility, resentment, and bad attitudes. They make us backsliders and ruin our testimonies. So let's hold that junk up to the Lord and let Him replace it with His love.

Lord, I praise You that as a Christian I can enjoy Your love, peace, and joy.

7/2/91

31

Trailing Arbutus: On the Rock

Bible Reading: 2 Samuel 22:1-7, 26-33

Let us make a joyful noise unto the rock of our salvation (Psalm 95:1b).

The trailing arbutus, otherwise known as mayflower or ground laurel, is the most fragrant of all wild flowers. The spicy-scented, small, pink or white tubular flowers of this hardy evergreen turn into red berries. The Massachusetts state flower grows on shady, rocky hillsides. Although it has tough stems and leaves, it is very difficult to transplant.

These plants grow on the rocks—and Christians grow on the Rock, the Lord. David often praised the Lord and called Him his rock, his fortress, his strength. He never failed to thank God and give Him the credit for bringing him through difficult times.

In Ephesians 2:20 our Lord Jesus Christ is called the "chief cornerstone" on which His church is built. Paul told the Corinthians that Christ was the spiritual Rock that had followed the Israelites in their desert wanderings.

If our lives are firmly planted on the Rock, Jesus Christ, then we shall not be moved, come what may. He will be our fortress, our deliverer, our shield, our refuge, our savior, our strength. He holds up all who trust in Him. Having all power, Jesus never fails. He has never failed me when I've needed Him. He has always given me all the strength and grace I've ever needed.

God is not partial. He gives strength, comfort, and grace to all of His children who trust and depend upon Him. Though you may be delicate in some respects, He can make you a fragrant flower and evergreen for Him.

Oh, Lord, I glory in the fact that You are my Rock, my strength, and power, and that You make my way perfect!

7/6/91

32

Mock Orange and Growing

Bible Reading: Ephesians 4:22-32

As newborn babes, desire the sincere milk of the word, that ye may grow thereby (1 Peter 2:2).

Mock orange shrubs make beautiful additions to the garden, with their profusion of large, white, fragrant double blooms in late spring or early summer. The Lewis mock orange is Idaho's state flower.

Wise gardeners prune the shrubs right after the flowering season is over. They thin out old wood to encourage new growth. They know also that if they trim new growth late in the season, they'll have few blossoms the following year, for it is the new growth that produces the flowers.

That reminds me of how the apostle Paul told the Ephesians to strip themselves of their old nature, to discard their fleshly unrenewed self with its deceitful lusts. He then told them to have a new mental and spiritual attitude, to "put on the new man." He went on to list the junk of the old nature that had to be pruned off, letting them know that those acts and attitudes grieved the Holy Spirit. He concluded by advising them to be kind, forgiving, helpful, and loving.

The apostle Peter gave similar advice in his first epistle (1 Peter 2:1). There he told Christians to crave the milk of the word, so that they might grow as a consequence. So the Lord has given us two excellent recipes for producing the sweet fragrance and beauty of Christ in our lives. If Christians delay pruning, however, their future growth in Christian graces will be delayed.

For joy, glory in the fact that when you received Christ as Savior, you became a new person. Like a snake sheds his skin, you can shed the old you and allow the new you to take control.

Lord, I rejoice that with Your help I can be a new person.

33

Lady's Slippers, Orchids, and Slow Growers

Bible Reading: Hebrews 5:5–6:3

Grow up into him who is the Head, that is, Christ (Ephesians 4:15b, NIV*).

I learned something I didn't know before: lady's slippers are members of the orchid family, which includes more than ten thousand species. Pink and white, the gorgeous, showy lady's slipper is Minnesota's state flower.

Orchids range in color from pink to purple, white, yellow, and orange. Most grow in

* *New International Version.*

the rich, moist soil of forest or bogs. I'll never forget the day I discovered a dainty pink one out in the forest near Ocean Gate. It was so unexpected to find it in such a place!

Orchids are formed differently from other flowers, their conspicuous feature being that one of their three petals is formed into a nectar-secreting lip for attracting bees and facilitating pollination. Wild orchids come up yearly from thick, fleshy roots. They grow slowly and are hard to transplant and difficult to grow from their miniscule seeds.

The Bible speaks of Christians growing in the grace and knowledge of the Lord. It also deals with slow-growing Christians like the Corinthians and the Hebrews. It's hard to grasp that even people in the early church, who were blessed by the ministry of the apostles, did not seem to be mature Christians. The writer of Hebrews, whom many believe to be the apostle Paul, was disappointed in the Hebrew Christians. "You're still in beginners' class," he seemed to say. "When are you going to go on and grow up as Christians?"

So it isn't surprising, is it, that today we find many in the church just like those early

Christians. They might be called the ABC Christians: Accepted the Lord, was Baptized, joined the Church . . . period.

What can we do to go further, to mature? Well, we have something today that most of those Christians didn't have: we have the whole New Testament in print, as well as the Old. Just as food for the body helps us to grow physically, so God's food for the soul, His Word, helps us to grow spiritually. As we learn His way and Word, we grow.

When I was working to help my husband go through Bible college, on my walk to and from work I would memorize Scriptures. I believe I laid in my mind about four hundred verses, and while I was doing this I was growing. Since then those verses have continued to contribute to my growth.

Another thing that helped me grow was life's school of sorrow, pain, loss, frustration, disappointment, and heartbreak. If you take those things to the Lord and trust Him all the way through them, you will come out knowing a lot more about Him and His way and His grace than you did before.

I've learned a lot through spending time in prayer, too, for it has been at such times that the Lord has communicated with me. Prayer also helps those baby Christians who still need to grow, for God will work in their lives in answer to our heartfelt prayers.

Praise the Lord for His provisions for spiritual growth! For the more we grow, the closer we are to enjoying Christ's abundant life.

Lord, help me to grow and be more like Jesus.

7/14/91

34

Apple Blossoms: Fruit

Bible Reading: Galatians 5:16-26

For the fruit of the Spirit is in all goodness and righteousness and truth (Ephesians 5:9).

In April my apple trees bloom, and they are breathtakingly beautiful. The crab apple tree is covered with deep pink blossoms, and my yellow delicious produces big white flowers with delicate pink buds all around. No wonder Michigan and Arkansas chose the apple blossom as their state flower.

Not only do these blossoms provide a treat for the eyes, but they produce fruit that pleases the body. My mother makes jelly out of the crab apples, and I put up apples aplenty for my freezer, as well as eating them out of hand.

Just as apple blossoms result in fruit, so should a true conversion to Jesus Christ result in fruit. For the apostle Paul wrote to the Corinthians that "by one Spirit we [Christians] were all baptized into one body" and "were all made to drink of one Spirit" (1 Corinthians 12:13, NASB). The Holy Spirit produces His fruit in the life of a person who has been born again, and it is beautiful.

It is said that an apple a day keeps the doctor away. Well, I firmly believe that being filled with the Spirit and His fruit is a powerful way to stay in good health. Why? Just look at the fruit of the Spirit: love, joy, peace, patience, kindness, goodness, faithfulness, gentleness, self-control. Can you see how having those qualities in your life would lead to a tranquil mind and life of faith, which in turn would result in physical, emotional, and mental health?

Paul spoke to the Galatians as if it were up to them as to whether they would choose to live in the flesh or walk in the Spirit. They were Christians, but evidently Paul had to warn them about the way some of them were living. We can't stay on the fence spiritually if we want to enjoy all the wonderful blessings of the fruit of the Spirit in our lives.

Apples are under attack from a number of sources. If I don't spray my apples at least several times, they get worms in them. If I don't remove all dead leaves and fruit on the ground, they get scab. Birds also feast on them if I don't get to them first!

We Christians are also under attack from evil spiritual forces as well as from our own flesh and the cares of life that assail. So our spiritual life needs to be nourished daily with good helpings of God's Word and prayer. It helps also to examine our lives for the dead leaves of "ho-hum rut" orthodoxy and "go-go" syndrome, not to mention actual sin. All these things may grieve or quench the Holy Spirit. When this happens, a Christian gets low on fruit!

But let us glory in the Lord that we can be filled with the fruit of the Spirit as we yield ourselves to Him! It's available right now!

Lord, fill me with Your Spirit. Help me to walk in the Spirit daily.

35

Hibiscus: Mallows and Musk

Bible Reading: Philippians 4:14-20

For we are unto God a sweet [fragrance] of Christ (2 Corinthians 2:15).

Hibiscus is the genus name for the more than two hundred species of trees, shrubs, and herbs of the mallow family, which is widely known for its decorative perennials, perfume, food plants, and beautifully colored tropical trees and shrubs. The hibiscus is Hawaii's state flower.

The rose mallow is one of the better known varieties; it particularly favors salt marshes. I have fond memories of riding on my bicycle along Ocean Gate's boardwalk

111

over a salt marsh full of the beautiful pink rose mallows. I'm also partial to the pretty yellow mallow that produces okra. I love to eat the pods raw off their stalks, or cooked in stews. And then there is the musk mallow, a native of India that is grown mostly for its seeds, which give a musky perfume.

All of this reminds me of Paul's telling the Corinthians that he and Timothy, who were spreading the gospel, had a sweet fragrance of Christ in their lives. I believe this is true of any Christian who truly lives Christ before others and tells them about Jesus and His love and sacrifice.

Paul also wrote to the Philippians about something that smelled sweet to God and was well-pleasing to Him: the sacrificial gift they sent to him to provide for his needs. I wonder how much happier we would be about giving to our church and missions if we truly realized how much the fragrant odor of cheerful giving pleases our Lord.

Those who go forth as missionaries for Christ delight the Lord with the fragrance of their sacrifice. Those who give to their support are also sweet to Him. We can glory in the privilege of doing something to please our Lord.

Lord, may I be a sweet fragrance of Christ in every area of my life.

7/23/91

36

Iris: Rainbow

Bible Reading: Psalm 34

There hath not failed one word of all his good promise (1 Kings 8:56b).

Iris is the Greek name for rainbow. It's easy to see how it got its name. Irises may come in two or more colors. Among their approximately two hundred species can be found all the colors of the rainbow, and then some: brilliant shades of yellow, blue, and purple; orange-copper, pink, red, wine, copper-brown, and white. The Louisiana iris resembles an orchid. Tennessee has chosen the gorgeous Siberian, with its deep, rich purple tones, as its state flower.

Each spring my purple, lavender, yellow, copper-edged, and white irises bloom. I think they are prettier than orchids.

Since iris means rainbow, let's consider the rainbow. God gave mankind His rainbow as a reminder of one of His greatest promises, that He would never send a universal flood on earth again. Both the prophet Ezekiel and the apostle John reported seeing a rainbow around God's throne. The rainbow makes me think of God's promises in general, and He has given us plenty of marvelous promises that outnumber the variety of irises.

Do we really believe God's promises? Psalm 34 is one of my favorite psalms because, like a rainbow full of gorgeous colors, it is full of God's life-changing promises. This psalm has often helped me as I've claimed one of its promises. In fact, when times of trouble have come, the Lord has given me various promises out of His Word. I can remember those times when He met my needs by the dates I wrote next to the promises He gave.

Do you have a need? Check the psalms for one of God's promises, claim it, and be-

lieve it. God is faithful. He keeps His beautiful promises with those who love and follow
Him. Now glory in that precious truth.

*Lord, thank You for all Your precious
promises and help me to trust in these and in
You.*

37

Lupines: All Kinds

Bible Reading: 1 John 4:7-15

Receive ye one another, as Christ also received us to the glory of God (Romans 15:7).

Lupines come in all kinds. The delicate, pea-type flowers of more than 150 species of lupines come in many shades of white, pink, red, maroon, purple, blue, violet, yellow, and combinations of colors. Differently colored lupines often grow in the same area.

Lupines may be annuals, biennials, or perennials. Some grow only a few inches above the ground; others grow eight feet tall. Lupines grow in fields, arid plains, and deserts. But some prefer moist soil by streams.

117

The bluebonnet, the Texas state flower, is a lupine.

Christians come in all kinds too. There are the outgoing, hearty, talkative kind; the strong-willed go-getters; the creative musical types; the plodding, dependable soldiers. There are the young, the middle-aged, the elderly. We have all kinds of backgrounds and heredities that tend to make us what we are. Some are baby Christians who must be handled with kid gloves; others are rocks who have weathered the storms. How can so many different types get along?

Unfortunately, they sometimes don't, because they don't understand one another and may have little tolerance for the idiosyncrasies of others. So we see Christians at odds with one another, as Paul saw in the Corinthian church. We all know how much this can hurt the work of our Lord.

Ah, but there is something grand we can glory in. Our Lord has made a provision for binding us together in understanding: it is His love that He will fill our hearts with if we'll let Him. His Word says that when we have this love for our diverse brothers and

118

sisters, it is a sign that we are truly born again.

Nevertheless, because we often fall short of loving because of anger, hurt pride, or inability to forgive one another, the Lord reminds us through His Word that we are to love one another.

Now think of those you don't understand or may not approve of in your church. Consider that if they have repented and received Christ as Savior, they are indeed your brothers and sisters whom Christ loved enough to die for, even as He did for you. Forgive. Pray for understanding and patience. Think of some way that you can show love toward these people—and do it.

Oh, then you will glory in the joy Christ gives you in your heart.

Lord, help me to truly love all my brothers and sisters.

38

Peony: Faithful Producer

Bible Reading: Colossians 1:9-14

Be not weary in well-doing (2 Thessalonians 3:13b).

When I look at a peony, I can't help but think of a beautiful gown full of ruffles. This aristocrat of the flower world is a perennial, putting out its fragrant red, pink, or white blossoms year after year with only a minimum of attention. It is Indiana's state flower.

Peonies may be planted in full sun or partial shade, but they often need some support. If more glorious blooms are desired, pinch off side buds, leaving only one.

What can we learn from the peony? We can be inspired to continue serving the Lord year after year, even as the peony produces its blessing of blooms year after year. Our Scripture encourages us to always lead a life worthy of the Lord, to be filled with His strength no matter what happens, to be always full of His joy. Do you know some Christians like that? Aren't they beautiful?

Some Christians go on like that for a while and then fall away. I know certain ones who did so because they felt they did not have the support of fellow Christians. Some of us may be able to stand alone, but most of us need support and encouragement. Let's remember that and help peony Christians to keep on standing and serving.

Jesus said that His Father prunes such branches so that they can bear more fruit (John 15:2). So if you are going through a painful pruning time, glory in the Lord because of how much more beautiful you will be for Jesus because of it. When you praise the Lord, it lifts your heart, no matter what the circumstances. That in turn will help to replace depression with joy!

Lord, help me walk worthy of You, be fruitful, faithful, and grow.

121

8/11/91

39

Peaches and Frost

Bible Reading: 1 Peter 1:3-8

*I am exceeding joyful in all our tribu-
lation (2 Corinthians 7:4b).*

Here in the northwestern corner of
South Carolina where I live, peach orchards
abound. My peach trees have produced some
delicious-tasting fruits. Before they do that,
they are covered with a gorgeous array of
pink flowers. I can well understand why the
peach blossom is Delaware's state flower.

A certain amount of freezing weather
during winter is necessary for a peach tree
to produce fruit. But one April two late frosts
struck just as many trees were flowering.
Some peach growers were almost wiped out.

A meeting was held to encourage the orchardists to grow alternate crops, such as corn and soybeans. I believe this whole matter has worked out for their advantage and survival, because since then we have experienced other late frosts in which peach crops have been destroyed.

We can glory in the Lord for pink-flowering trees and delicious peaches. And we can glory in Him for the "frosts" He allows in our lives. Just as cold spells help peach trees produce fruit, so trials help us Christians produce fruit unto God (Hebrews 12:11). And just as those late frosts have worked for the future good of the peach growers, so late frosts work for our future good.

Through trials we can experience God's grace, comfort, help, and answers to prayer —if we look to Him. As others see the strength and faith we have in our trials, it testifies to them of God's grace. It can open doors for us to witness for our Lord, and perhaps even influence others to come to Him.

Unfortunately, some Christians become bitter toward God and other people when they go through trials. This bitterness creates a wall between them and the Lord, as well as between them and the people they won't forgive. It mars their testimony and service for the Lord. They may have a feeling of discontent, a lack of peace, and not know why. "Bitter City" is a slummy place to live— it's really in the dumps.

What can we do if such a continuing frost has blighted our lives? Forgive. Repent. Pray Psalm 51:1-13. Let God produce His fruit in us.

Lord, help me to rejoice in You always.

40

Calochortus: Beautiful Grass

Bible Reading: Isaiah 40:1-11

What is your life? It is even a vapor, that appeareth for a little time, and then vanisheth away (James 4:14).

The genus name for the more than thirty species of *Calochortus* comes from the Greek words *kalos* and *chortos,* which together mean "beautiful grass." Of the lily family, and closely related to tulips, these are natives of western North America that have grass-like leaves and produce showy yellow, red, white, and lilac flowers which are often darker toward their centers.

Many people might better recognize this type of flower by the names mariposa lily or sego lily. The latter, a white tulip-like flower, is Utah's state flower, and its edible forms once were considered a delicacy by the Indians.

The prophet Isaiah compared mankind with grass and flowers. He declared that all men are like grass that withers, and their glory like flowers that fade. Then he said, "But the word of our God shall stand forever" (Isaiah 40:8b). Peter quoted him in the New Testament. James gave a similar message, that our lives are like a vapor that vanishes away.

In one church I attended we used to sing a song, "This World Is Not My Home." The gist of the song was that we are just briefly passing through on our way to eternity, that our treasures are laid up in heaven.

For Albert E. Brumley, who wrote that song, and for many who have sung it, that is probably true. It should be true of all of us who claim the name of Christ. But I'm afraid many professing Christians today have their eyes more on amassing earthly treasures rather than heavenly. However, just as the sego lily's grasslike foliage and flowers fade and die, so does all mankind. We can't take it with us—we can only send it ahead by living for Jesus.

In God's gallery of heroes and heroines of faith, Hebrews 11, the writer declares by inspiration of God that these people confessed that they were strangers and pilgrims on the earth, that they desired a better country, a heavenly one. He said that God is not ashamed to be called their God, and He has prepared for them a city. That chapter is well worth reading if we wish to appreciate how men and women of true faith lived.

But just think: those people didn't have the story of the gospel as we have it. They didn't have Bibles to read in their homes, and the New Testament with accounts of God's Son on earth and its other valuable Scriptures had not yet been written. Nor did they have the indwelling Spirit as born-again Christians have Him. Do they not then put many of us to shame with their faith?

Our lives on earth are brief, but what we do with them will vitally affect our entire eternity. Our bodies will die; our spirits will either go to be with the Lord or go to the burning pit, depending on whether or not we have received Jesus Christ as our Savior. If we are Christians, we will stand before the judgment seat of Christ to account for ourselves. There what we have done on earth will either be deemed hay, wood, and stubble, or worthy of eternal rewards.

It is never too late for us to give our hearts to Christ, to start living for Him, to set our affections on heaven and begin laying up treasures there. Praise the Lord for this blessed truth.

O Lord, help me to make my life count for Your glory.

41

Cacti

Bible Reading: John 15:9-17

*Hitherto have ye asked nothing in my
name: ask, and ye shall receive, that
your joy may be full (John 16:24).*

When my family and I lived in southwestern Colorado, we enjoyed picnics out on
the wild, arid bluffs that overlooked the Do-
lores River.

Stunted trees and weird foliage dotted
the dry land. But some time after a gully-
washer or two would flash across the land,
beautiful waxy flowers would appear—cacti
of all kinds and colors. How strange to see
those gorgeous decorations on their spiny,
leafless bodies!

Cacti thrive on lots of sunshine, sandy soil, and little water. They adorn otherwise dreary places. The Christmas cactus makes a graceful house plant. The saguaro cactus provides Arizona's state flower.

Like a cactus, a Christian thrives on lots of sunshine—let's call that the joy that Jesus promised His followers. That joy causes us to bubble over with a cheerful spirit that blesses and lifts up others. That joy lifts us into a spirit of praise and out of depression and doldrums.

Have you been enjoying the joy of the Lord? If not, would you like to? Jesus tied the fullness of His joy to our abiding in Him. That means having a continual, intimate relationship with our Master. Like branches, we have been grafted into Christ, the Vine. He is our source of joy, power, strength, and fruitfulness. Glory in Him whenever you think of it.

With Christ in our lives we can adorn otherwise dreary places. Gritty spots cause us to thrive. Like the great barrel cactus, rivers of living water flow out of us to quench the spiritual thirst of others.

Part of our joy comes from seeing prayers answered, as we ask in our Master's name. For the Father loves us, because we love and obey His Son (see John 16:27).

Lord, help me to love You more and abide in You.

42

Rhododendrons

Bible Reading: Psalm 30

Weeping may endure for a night, but joy cometh in the morning (Psalm 30:5).

Rhododendrons are magnificently showy flowers that make great front-yard displays in the spring. Their size varies from six inches to forty feet high, and they love acid soil. Bell-shaped, they come in every color of the rainbow. They thrive in partial shade, as do azaleas—which are really rhododendrons. Two varieties of rhododendron are the state flowers of Washington and West Virginia.

Spring comes early in Greenville, South Carolina, where I live. Forsythias bloom in January, camellias and crocuses in February. Everything gets ready to bloom—including the row of rhododendrons across the front of my house. When a hard freeze doesn't hit in April, a gorgeous array of fuchsia-colored rhododendron blossoms splash the front of my light yellow house with exotic trim. But quite often that late freeze knocks out all the blossoms except those between the bushes and the building!

Sometimes "hard freezes" hit us, too—and they can knock out our blooming beauty that reflects Christ in our lives. These freezes may consist of losing a loved one, a job, a home, or our health. A broken marriage or a wayward child may devastate us. Like the rhododendrons, we may sail along just fine until the trial strikes. Then Gloomsville City has nothing on us.

Some of us may lose our faith in the Lord. We may fall away from the church, stop serving, giving, and praying, and become miserable people who make others miserable, too. But we do have a choice as to how we take our "hard freeze."

133

The frost-hit rhododendrons do bloom in their sheltered area—and the following spring they may come out in all their glory. We Christians may be temporarily snowed under by our trial, but if we hang in there, looking to our Lord and trusting Him no matter what, He will bring us through to a new dimension of spiritual beauty that has been enhanced by our suffering and what we have learned of our Lord's loving concern and sustaining grace.

Oh, Lord, I do trust You. I choose Your way of faith, peace, and joy!

43

Petunias, Loneliness, and Faith

Bible Reading: Hebrews 11:24-40

These all died in faith . . . and confessed that they were strangers and pilgrims on the earth (Hebrews 11:13).

Many home gardeners, including myself, love the graceful, many-colored petunias that bloom all summer. I found that when a petunia springs up by itself it reverts to original form and color, which is not as attractive as the hybrids, though its fragrance is much sweeter. The fancy petunias we have today were hybridized from two original species and come in all kinds of mixed colors, in singles, doubles, ruffled, crisped, marked with stars, eyes, and margins.

Some years ago a song naming the petunia was popular—"I'm a lonely little petunia in an onion patch...." Sometimes as Christians we may indeed feel that way. We may be the only ones in our families, neighborhoods, or work places who love Jesus and try to follow Him. For that reason those around us may not understand us and might even make things unpleasant for us. How can we handle it without feeling sorry for ourselves and miserable?

The Bible says that we who follow the Lord are strangers and pilgrims in this world. It's not our home. Fellow believers who lived during Old Testament times only saw the promise afar, yet by faith they lived and suffered for the Lord. We now know the whole way of salvation and of how our Lord Himself left heaven's glory to become a stranger and pilgrim on earth for our sakes.

We know that He too must have felt lonely at times, for even His followers often didn't understand Him and eventually betrayed or deserted Him. So our Savior understands every heartache, every pang of loneliness we have—and He can give us all the grace and guidance we need.

The apostle Paul wrote his spiritual son Timothy that all in Asia had turned away from him when he was a prisoner. But according to the letter to the Philippians, he had learned to rejoice in the Lord always. That surely must have lifted him above the depression and lonely feeling his circumstances prompted in him.

I have found that praising the Lord and rejoicing in Him has lifted me up many such times. I may not feel like rejoicing in the Lord, but I start doing it anyway, thinking of the things I have to be thankful for. In a few minutes I find that I am rejoicing from my heart, and the gloom is dispelled.

We are strangers and pilgrims in this world and have a far better country called heaven to look forward to, just as those saints of old did. There we will find fellowship with the Lord and with our true brothers and sisters for eternity. God will wipe away all tears; there will be no more sorrow or death or crying. Look up—and praise the Lord!

Oh, Lord, I glory in You, my redeemer, my rock, my strength, my master, and my friend!

State Flowers

Alaska—Forget-me-not
Alabama—Goldenrod
Arkansas—Apple blossom
Arizona—Saguaro cactus

California—California golden poppy
Colorado—Blue columbine
Connecticut—Mountain laurel

Delaware—Peach blossom

Florida—Orange blossom

Georgia—Cherokee rose

Hawaii—Hibiscus

Idaho—Lewis mock orange
Illinois—Violet
Indiana—Peony
Iowa—Wild rose

Kansas—Sunflower
Kentucky—Goldenrod

Louisiana—Magnolia

Maine—Pinecone
Massachusetts—Trailing arbutus
Minnesota—Showy lady's slipper
Michigan—Apple blossom
Maryland—Black-eyed Susan
Mississippi—Magnolia
Missouri—Hawthorn
Montana—Bitterroot

Nebraska—Goldenrod
New Jersey—Violet
Nevada—Sagebrush
New Hampshire—Lilac
New Mexico—Yucca
New York—Rose
North Carolina—Flowering dogwood
North Dakota—Wild prairie rose

Ohio—Scarlet carnation
Oregon—Oregon grape
Oklahoma—Mistletoe

Pennsylvania—Mountain laurel

Rhode Island—Violet

South Carolina—Yellow jessamine
South Dakota—American pasqueflower

Tennessee—Siberian iris
Texas—Bluebonnet

Utah—Sego lily

Vermont—Red clover
Virginia—Flowering dogwood

Washington—Rhododendron
West Virginia—Rhododendron maximum
Wisconsin—Violet
Wyoming—Painted cups